RING ROUND THE MOON

JEAN ANOUILH

RING ROUND THE MOON

A Charade with Music

Translated by

CHRISTOPHER FRY

With a preface by

PETER BROOK

New York

OXFORD UNIVERSITY PRESS

1950

PREFACE

By Peter Brook

WHEN I saw *L'Invitation au Château* in Paris, I had an appointment at midnight in the Champs-Elysées. The curtain, of course, had gone up very late, the intervals seemed interminable, and long before the last act I had to slip away. The performance on the whole was uninspired, yet the fragment I saw was tantalizing, there seemed an enchanting mood hidden away behind it, and I was in a fever for a copy of the script.

The next morning, again in the Champs-Elysées, I ran into Bébé Bérard. He was shuffling along in his slippers, his beard tucked into his open-necked shirt like a scarf. "Have you seen *L'Invitation au Château*?" I asked. Bérard sighed. "Ah," he said, "what a chance for a designer. . . ."

Thank God, Oliver Messel felt the same thing. But that's to anticipate. To put on a foreign play in London, it's not enough to have read it—though I did the next day—nor to have a management interested—Tennents' were more than interested—nor to have a wonderful designer, nor a lot of actors. All these things are nothing, they neither exist, nor have any chance of existing, without an adaptation of the play that recaptures its quality in English.

This matter of adaptation is one of our greatest nightmares. Although Shakespeare is almost improved in German, and Chekhov is wonderful in French, our language is somehow as insular as our people, and it fights viciously against translators. Every season, plays successful abroad fail in London, their flops have a monotonous regularity, and although the cause is at times the producer or the cast,

5

mostly it is in the change of language. When a play is written in a realistic style, the problem is acute but not insuperable. It is then a question of finding the conversational equivalent, the parallel idiom, colloquialism for colloquialism, slang for slang. But Anouilh is a stylist, he has a manner and a way of phrasing in which much of his charm lies. To translate Anouilh is no matter of matching chat with chat: it demands re-creation, a re-shaping of ideas into phrases that have an English elegance and grace.

This recapturing of a French style has been achieved hardly more than a handful of times in English literature. Molière and Racine have defied a thousand adaptations. Only Otway, perhaps, in a century when for a brief moment English speech and manners approached those of France— in his hardly known translations of *Bérénice* and *Les Fourberies de Scapin*—succeeded.

I approached the task of getting Anouilh recaptured in English with trepidation. When, a few years ago, we had wanted to do Sartre's *Huis Clos*, we had had to reject eight translations. We were in final despair when suddenly the skies opened and a ninth appeared, which was brilliant, and the answer to all our prayers.

Christopher Fry drove us to final despair. He seemed the ideal person for the job. He was already clearly the best word-juggler of all. Also, he had shown proof of his abilities by a piece of nonsense he had translated, in *Twopence Coloured*. Although it only lasted the few instants that a revue sketch is allowed, it was artificial, witty and completely French. But—such is the way of things and writers— Christopher Fry said "No." He read the play, was interested, but none the less, was too hard at work. Entreaties did not move him. Fry appreciated Anouilh, but preferred to observe Venus. So, many months passed with any prospect of staging *L'Invitation au Château* growing fainter and

6

fainter. No other writer was right for this particular play. Then, once again the skies opened, the *deus ex machina* appeared. Christopher Fry, having finished the first act of *Venus Observed*, got stuck. He discovered he didn't know what happened next. It's curious to think how much can hinge on an accident, how this edition, the success of *Ring Round the Moon*, the livelihood of its whole company, and perhaps even the final shape of *Venus*, all owe themselves to this sudden impediment in a muse's flow.

I remember sitting with Fry on the Roman mound overlooking his Shipton-under-Wychwood cottage, and being told the story of the first act of *Venus Observed*. An observatory. An eclipse. And then what happens? I don't know. Perhaps something in a decaying temple by a lake. A few weeks' change from his own play seemed a wonderful idea, the idea of translating became palatable. *L'Invitation au Château* was saved.

The moment Christopher Fry began work on the script we all breathed more freely. But although the quality of the writing seemed guaranteed, the success of Anouilh's play was still much in the balance. Anouilh writes plays for performance rather than for paper. His literary quality is that of theatre literature, the elegance of his dialogue appears when it is spoken by comedians in the rhythm of a comic scene. His first play, *Le Bal des Voleurs*, was called a comédie-ballet, and he conceives his plays as ballets, as patterns of movement, as pretexts for actor's performances. Unlike so many present-day playwrights who are the descendants of a literary school, and whose plays are animated novels, Anouilh is in the tradition of the *commedia dell' arte*. His plays are recorded improvisations. Like Chopin, he preconceives the accidental and calls it an impromptu. He is a poet, but not a poet of words: he is a poet of words-acted, of scenes-set, of players-performing.

7

When the scenery was designed, the actors at work, the scenes beginning to come to life, we realized that an English audience might have difficulty in catching the style of the play. After all, the *commedia dell' arte* is little known here, the idiom is unfamiliar. We had to find a sub-title to make it all clear. But what? A comedy? A farce? A ballet? They all had the wrong connotations. Then Fry found the answer. "Call it a 'Charade with Music' " he suggested. So the reader, too, would do worse than to keep this description in mind, and read this play with sense of theatre and imagination alert. The written play is Anouilh's shorthand for a play performed, and the reader should try to animate the characters until he has them playing and dancing round the ferns and under the twinkling lights of a winter garden. The reader must be his own producer and stage his own charade. Believe me, it's an enchanting game.

This play was first presented at the Globe Theatre, London, by Tennent Productions Ltd. (in association with the Arts Council of Great Britain) on January 26th, 1950:

JOSHUA, *a crumbling butler*

HUGO, *a young man about town*

FREDERIC, *his brother, in love with*

DIANA MESSERSCHMANN,
engaged to Frederic, secretly in love with Hugo

LADY INDIA, *Messerschmann's mistress, secretly in love with*

PATRICE BOMBELLES,
Messerschmann's secretive secretary

MADAME DESMERMORTES, *Aunt to Hugo, Frederic and Lady India*

CAPULAT, *her faded companion*

MESSERSCHMANN, *Diana's father, a melancholy millionaire*

ROMAINVILLE, *a lepidopterist, patron of*

ISABELLE, *a ballet dancer*

HER MOTHER, *a teacher of the pianoforte*

A GENERAL

FOOTMEN

SCENE

The play takes place in a winter-garden, in spring

ACT ONE

SCENE 1

A rococo winter-garden; glass and wrought-iron; yellow plush curtains and green plants. It looks out on to a wide expanse of park. (Enter JOSHUA, *a butler, and* HUGO, *a young man-about-town, smoking a fat cigar.)*

HUGO.   And how about last night, Joshua? Did the same thing happen?

JOSHUA.   I'm sorry I can't deny it, Mr. Hugo, but the same thing did.

HUGO.   My brother slept all night under her window?

JOSHUA.   Yes, Mr. Hugo—under both her windows. For five nights now Mr. Frederic has gone to bed in a rhododendron bush: you know, sir, the one on the south side of the west wing, beside that statue they call Calliope, a classical character, sir. Every morning the housemaid has found his bed unrumpled, and the gardener has found the rhododendrons rumpled. Well, it gives them a jolt, Mr. Hugo, as who wouldn't it? I try to make light of it, so as to keep them in the dark: but one day they'll talk and Madam will know all about it.

HUGO.   Have you ever been in love, Joshua?

JOSHUA.   Now, sir, think: I've been in service with Madam for thirty years; I'm too old.

HUGO.   But before that?

JOSHUA.   I was too young.

HUGO.   Mine's the age for it, Joshua. I fall in love as a matter of routine. But not ludicrously like my brother.

11

JOSHUA. No, sir. Mr. Frederic hasn't your style at all, sir.

HUGO. And yet we're the same age. It's odd, isn't it?

JOSHUA. You're ten minutes older, sir, remember that.

HUGO. Yes, I know. But who would have thought that those ten minutes would have taught me so much about women?

JOSHUA. The young lady knows she can do what she likes with your brother, sir.

HUGO. She may think she knows. But—I've schemed a scheme.

JOSHUA. I'm glad to hear that, Mr. Hugo.

HUGO. I got up early this morning because I've decided to take action. This dawn is the dawn of the unexpected. What's the time?

JOSHUA. Twelve o'clock, Mr. Hugo.

HUGO. By twelve-thirty, Joshua, I shall begin to loom big on the horizon.

JOSHUA. Oh, and Mr. Hugo, sir—I attempted to explain away the rhododendrons, sir, by informing the gardener that a wolf had been observed making depredations in the vicinity, sir. I told him not to mention this, sir, on the grounds that it might occasion the guests a measure of comprehensible alarm, sir. . . . Thank you, sir.

Exit HUGO. *Enter* FREDERIC. *It is the same actor.*

FREDERIC. Joshua!

JOSHUA. Mr. Frederic?

FREDERIC. Has Miss Diana come down yet?

JOSHUA. Not yet, Mr. Frederic.

FREDERIC. Do I look tired, Joshua?

JOSHUA. If I may be allowed to be frank, yes, you do, sir.

FREDERIC. But you're quite mistaken, you know. I've never slept better.

12

JOSHUA. I think I ought to tell you, sir, the gardener's intending to set wolf-traps in the rhododendrons.

FREDERIC. Never mind, Joshua. I'll sleep in the azaleas.

JOSHUA. And the housemaid, sir, the one who looks after the west wing, she has been making remarks of horrified dissatisfaction. She came to see me quite ready to drop.

FREDERIC. Tell her, next time, to drop into my bed, if she would be so good, and untidy it herself.

JOSHUA. Oh, Mr. Frederic!

FREDERIC. Why not? She's very charming. And when she's unmade it sufficiently she will be able to make it again, and everything will seem to be just as usual.

JOSHUA. Very good, Mr. Frederic.

Exit JOSHUA. *Enter* DIANA.

FREDERIC. Diana! How good to see you again. It's been like a lifetime since yesterday.

DIANA (*stopping and looking at him*). Which one of you is it now?

FREDERIC (*reproachfully*). Oh, Diana; that's not a nice thing to ask me!

DIANA. Ah yes, it is you. You're looking at me like a little lost dog again. Did you get up on the wrong side of the rhododendrons? At first you looked so triumphant I thought you were your brother.

FREDERIC. If you prefer him to me, I shall go away and die.

DIANA. Dear Frederic! You know I should only mistake you by accident. You're so alike.

FREDERIC. Our hearts aren't alike.

DIANA. No, that's true. But imagine me alone in the park one evening: I hear the twigs cracking behind me and

13

what sounds like your step: two arms go round me, and
they feel like your arms: a mouth kisses me, and it feels
like your mouth. How am I to have time to make sure it's
the right heart, Frederic?

FREDERIC. But, Diana, I've never put my arms round you
in the park.

DIANA. Are you sure?

FREDERIC. Perfectly sure. Diana! It was my brother,
looking like me on purpose! It was my double, double-
crossing me again! I must find him: I've got to speak to
him!

DIANA (*laughing and stopping him*). Now, dear, dear, *dear*,
dear, *dear* Frederic! Don't go rushing to conclusions. I
made it up. No one's been kissing me.

FREDERIC (*hanging his head*).   I beg your pardon, Diana.
I completely believe you. But if Hugo loved you, I should
kill myself.

DIANA. That would be terrible. I should never be sure
which of you was dead. (*She is pensive a moment.*) Of
course it would be a great help to your brother; he would
only have to drop a few tears for you at the funeral, and
then come and whisper in my ear, "Ssh: don't tell anyone!
They've made a great mistake. This is really Hugo's
funeral!" How should I answer that?

FREDERIC. But you couldn't be deceived for a moment,
could you? If I were so exactly like Hugo, in word and
thought and deed, I should *be* Hugo.

DIANA. Yes, that's true.

FREDERIC (*after a pause*). Diana, it's Hugo you love!
Good-bye.

DIANA. Are you mad? I hate him. Kiss me.

FREDERIC (*lost*). Diana!

DIANA. Kiss me, you lost dog, and I'll find your way home
for you.

14

FREDERIC. I love you.

DIANA. I love you, too, Frederic.

They kiss.

I suppose you're quite sure you're not Hugo? He's capable of absolutely anything.

They go.

Enter LADY INDIA *and* PATRICE BOMBELLES.

PATRICE. Anything! Anything! He's capable of absolutely anything.

LADY INDIA. But, dear heart, how could he suspect us? We've been so careful.

PATRICE. I tell you, I wouldn't trust that fellow Hugo an inch. Yesterday he giggled at me. Quite noticeably, as I went past him. Why should he have giggled if he didn't know all about us?

LADY INDIA. When did he giggle?

PATRICE. Last night, on the terrace, after dinner.

LADY INDIA. Last night? We were all there together. He choked himself with cigar smoke. He was coughing.

PATRICE. He was coughing to disguise his giggle, but that didn't deceive me for a moment.

LADY INDIA. Anyway, why should this young man, who has nothing to do with me, giggle because he's found out we're having an affair?

PATRICE. Never mind why; mistrust him. To begin with there's this fantastic likeness to his brother.

LADY INDIA. He can't help that.

PATRICE. My dear Dorothy! If he had any sense of propriety, he would never allow it to go on. He revels in it; he copies his brother's clothes.

LADY INDIA. No, dear, Frederic copies his.

PATRICE. Well, it's the same thing. Now, I have eight brothers——

15

LADY INDIA. And they all look exactly like you?

PATRICE. Not at all.

LADY INDIA. I see; then it doesn't help to convince me that this boy would say anything to Messerschmann.

PATRICE. *Say* anything, no; but little jokes and innuendoes when we're all in the drawing-room, yes; a mysterious chuckle in the middle of a meal, or a giggle like the one you thought was choking him with cigar-smoke; yes, most certainly.

LADY INDIA. Little jokes and chuckles will pass right over Messerschmann's head. He suffers from terribly poor reception.

PATRICE. It's we who would have a poor reception if once he knew. Don't forget, you're his mistress and I'm his private secretary. We're both completely dependent on your magnate.

LADY INDIA (*reproachfully*). Dearest heart, you use the most curious words.

PATRICE. Magnate?

LADY INDIA. No.

PATRICE. Private secretary?

LADY INDIA. No. (*She leans against him.*) Patrice, darling, I know I give him the pleasure of paying my bills, and every night I let him trail along to my room to kiss my hand; but that means nothing, and you mean everything.

PATRICE (*desperately*). Dorothy! We're in the winter-garden——

LADY INDIA. On a lovely spring morning.

PATRICE. The season is immaterial! All this glass! Everyone can see us! We're completely exposed.

LADY INDIA. Danger! Oh, that's wonderful; I love it; I like being mad more than anything. Did I ever tell you about the evening in Monte Carlo when I went to a little

16

dockside café, absolutely naked except for a cloak and my
diamonds? Quite alone, too, amongst all those drunken
brutes.

PATRICE. At Monte Carlo?

LADY INDIA. A little café where the croupiers used to sip
a secret Bock between sessions. I just smiled to see how
their hands shook when they raised their glasses. . . . So
let him come, let him catch us, let him murder us! I shall
drive him off with a lash of contempt! . . . It will be
magnificent!

PATRICE. Yes.

LADY INDIA. Don't forget you belong to a most distin-
guished family, Patrice, and I, after all, am Lady India.
He should be very grateful that we take the trouble to
infuriate him. Money isn't everything.

They go.

Enter MME. DESMERMORTES, *in a wheel-chair, pushed
by her companion,* CAPULAT, *and* HUGO.

MME. DESMER. Money is nothing! Oodles, oodles,
oodles? Whatever do you mean, Hugo, that Mr. Messerschmann has oodles?

HUGO. He's as rich as Crœsus.

MME. DESMER. Oh, I see—but whatever does he do with
it all?

HUGO. Eats noodles.

MME. DESMER. You're being absolutely too playful,
Hugo.

HUGO. It's quite true. At every meal, without butter or
salt, and drinks water.

MME. DESMER. How very spectacular. And you tell me
that Dorothy India is ruining him?

HUGO. She would be, if anyone could be, but there's too
much of it even for her.

17

MME. DESMER (*remembering* CAPULAT). You're a scandal-monger, Hugo. You forget I'm your aunt, and India's aunt. I won't listen to you. I'm an elderly woman, and I never listen to anyone. Capulat, go and look for my handkerchief.

CAPULAT *exits*.

Now, between ourselves, do you really imagine he's keeping her?

HUGO. Between ourselves, without a shadow of doubt.

MME. DESMER. It's monstrous, Hugo; humiliating.

HUGO. Utterly monstrous, but, between ourselves, why humiliating?

MME. DESMER. She is a FitzHenry! And through me, a Desmermortes. If only your uncle Antony were alive it would kill him. Hugo, people are so unkind; they will think I invited Dorothy and this nabob at the same time on purpose. They'll say I'm a party to it. So should I.

HUGO. Everyone knows you invited Mr. Messerschmann and his daughter because Frederic asked you to. Frederic is going to announce his engagement to Diana tomorrow.

MME. DESMER. Yes. There's another puppy-witted piece of folly! Fancy becoming so infatuated with that girl he even has to ask her to marry him! When he was little he always looked so sad and resigned when he came to kiss me on Christmas morning. I used to call him St. Pancras. And now the poor lamb's to be sacrificed. Can you bear to think of him being delivered over, gagged and bound, in his morning coat and gardenia, to this Diana Messerschmann and her millions?

HUGO. No, Aunt.

MME. DESMER. No, I should think not. If it had been you, it would have been different. I love it when the lamb

18